Unbecoming Human

Milton Cruz

ISBN 979-8-89043-618-4 (paperback)
ISBN 979-8-89130-945-6 (hardcover)
ISBN 979-8-89043-619-1 (digital)

Christian Faith Publishing
832 Park Avenue
Meadville, PA 16335
www.christianfaithpublishing.com

Printed in the United States of America

I want to dedicate this book to my children and all the students whom I have touched in one way or another.

Prologue

Human friend:

*The title of this book is a call for all humans who have little or much
ability to analyze their present mental, spiritual, and physical status.*

*It gets my attention to express the irresponsible actions
of the present leaders who take time off in the middle
of the socioeconomic status of our people.*

*Neglected opportunities to collaborate with the people in most
need of personal, emotional, and political assurance.*

*After seeing political leaders take time off when
citizens are going through historical winter
storms, economic chaos, and a clear invasion of undocumented
people from all over the world, it only makes me reflect on
why this is happening in our country and our world.*

*Let's stop the race for superiority. Let's recognize our
own limits as creators. Let's stimulate others to achieve a
positive attitude toward what can bring harmony
and reject everything that contributes to division, indifference, and apathy.*

*A continuous effort in finding negative things will
destroy all chances for cohesion and harmony.*

The survival of the fittest represents our survival with the fittest. In this book, you can identify yourself with familiar thoughts and ideas that might have come across your mind.

Things that keep us apart are race or ethnicity, social class, economic status, educational status, professional level, technical and personal experience, personal religious affiliation, or lack of it.

The moment has come for everyone to reflect and realize that if our leaders do not prove to be fit for what we elect them, we must stop unbecoming humans from starting all over again. This time, putting aside all the things that keep us apart and convey a mutual understanding of agreement for prosperity without blocking the needed opportunities to improve among ourselves.

The ones opposing this should not be ignored and have them live in their own selected zones of self-destructive society.

Will this resolve our problems? No, but it will keep us from its negative rhetorical influence.

Lifting our self-esteem and human image will improve and allow us to share our differences with dignity and pride.

We can celebrate being different and still being able to accomplish anything and everything that can improve our lifestyle.

In the following sections, you will find thoughts that you can connect with.

You can adapt any or lots of these thoughts and have a restart in your personal journey. I hope you can accomplish such objectives.

Let's take the required time to treat ourselves to a personal introspection and self-improvement.

We could succeed in our human, social, economic, and spiritual life.

What happened to our humanity?

Thank you for bringing me back to it.

Your human friend, Milton

Canceling Our Past

If we cancel our past, we will have no future.
Touch, sight, hearing, smell, and taste, our needed senses
will be lost as a constant reminder of our inability
to understand the purpose of humans.
The only thing left permanently is the present.
Regretting our past only makes us repeat it permanently.

Let Us Create Chaos!

You can make something look bad, and it will turn bad.
You can make something look good, and it will turn good.
You can make something good bad or make something bad good.
You can make confusion look clear confusion.
And men said, "LET US CREATE CHAOS!"
Shortly after creation, men said:
"Let us break creation and the established order of things."

Reverse every law of physics and nature.
Let us not hold balance about anything.
Let chaos be the norm in everything until we reach the infinite.
Let us distort everything created!
The uniformity of languages so no one can
understand one another.
And we will have absolute control
on everything.

Confusion

The detour road of confusion.
Are you lost?
Cannot find your way?
Follow the signs of your instinct!
Still lost?
Is it a one-way or a multiple-way path?
Whichever is, you must be determined and get out of confusion.
You can make confusion look clear or clarify confusion.

Controversial

*A word for
Unhappiness.*

*Not willing to settle.
Any differences.*

Deception Versus Depression

The great deception of the COVID-19 virus of
the twenty-first century year 2020.

Living in a society filled with corrupt politicians, a clueless
educational system, spiritual bankruptcies, financial insecurities,
and parental lack of responsibilities toward their family and children.

Things learned from this crisis:
We are licensed to live at the time of conception.

Inflated egos can cause problems,
inability to treat others with respect.

Stop being selfish to attend to others.
Reaffirm human dignity.

Avoid depression and take over your life.

Parents who took off their job during the pandemic

should resume their job activities of being productive once more.

There is nothing more rewarding than to
contribute to our society.

Those not willing to return to a productive society will stand out for
their own reasons and believe that it can only bring destruction to all.

As for the empty streets in major cities we see on
TV, do not let your mind wander in them.

There is at stake and more to unleash from the
inventive mind of we the people.

And just as every surface is sanitized, we should sanitize our spirit
of creativity and let it guide us to realize that we will reemerge:
victorious of this temporary failure.

Let us name the failures and look not to repeat them again.

I am happy to see the people at warehouses buying
merchandise to improve their homes and properties.

The people have spoken; they believe in and
sustain our liberties by being free.

Let us celebrate our God-given rights: freedom of
speech, freedom to assembly, freedom of the press,
freedom to bear arms, and freedom of religion.

Let us consecrate our liberties to create an
environment of peace, not resentment.

We are a great nation capable of creating, learning, leading,
and implementing solutions for our people's needs.

Let us stay alert for those among us who promote big government
(oligarchs) instead of a representative government that takes seriously the
people's needs and do not waste time on petty
and insensitive personal gain.

We should not allow government representatives
to become filthy rich during

their tenure. Their fortune should be a derivative of the nation's wealth. Never increase the national debt unless is the last resource available to defend it from enemies' attacks or natural disasters.

Neither of those we control are expressions of nature itself or the jealousy of internal and external forces that impede or oppose our stable ambition of prosperity through the diversity of our human and natural resources.

Obeying rules helps us to survive mentally and physically. The defiant ones only expose everyone to the dangers of indifference or desire to expose their bravery in challenging times, taking the chance for failure or success.

The COVID-19 aid wants to show that we, the people, need the government's financial help to survive the present crisis.

The only solution offered by the government is to follow their rules.

Shut up and obey!

We do not have the ability to solve problems!

This I call submission and relinquishment of our freedom and liberties.

Just imagine a circle with twelve sides. It could not be named a circle because circles do not have sides.

But in this present situation of COVID-19 going around, this circle of solutions is like having to stop in twelve unusual places to complete one cycle of nonproductive answers.

If this reminds you of the Congress, you are correct. How much gets carried out in a twelve-month cycle? This confirms the theory of the twelve-angle circle.

*It does not and cannot be, as the US Congress
cannot get anything for us, the people.*

*I need to talk about trade skills. I think and wish that we could go to
the old way of trading goods instead of using our present currency.*

*The only thing that can be transferable are goods coming
from a well-integrated trade of goods and services,
fair to the demand and needs of the people or society.*

*The educational programs should emphasize basic knowledge and trade
practices that could benefit and supply the most required services.*

*Science should be relegated to support and not defy
the ingenuity of the human mind products.*

This entire article is to show that I am not depressed or deceived.

*I am aware of my surroundings and willing to help
in restoring our old American way of life.*

Let us get rid of all the hypocrites and begin again!

Destroying Ourselves!

Building

Destroying

Rebuilding

Destroying cycle again

Questioning ourselves, What happened?

Is it an endless pattern?

Does it have a positive and permanent end?

Devaluation of the American Revolution

There are challenges in a revolution.

Figuratively, revolutions originate from a need
for changes to improve the status quo.

When the main concept of its design is lost, or abandoned, it
goes through a buyer's remorse, which enhances and creates
the devaluation of everything already achieved.

This could be said about our own revolution for
independence from the British Empire.

Nowadays, those who have come to our country by
any means will face the moment when
they will ask themselves if they made the right decision.

If they did not contribute to their countries of origin through a
genuine revolution, they could partake in our devolution.

It will be a complicated situation. Our people demanding devolution
and the newcomers demanding to be part of our earlier revolution.

All originated and started in the United States
of America, the cradle of our present
democracy.

For how much longer? It is extremely hard to figure this
out, but surely it is happening under our noses.

Buyers' remorse is an act of insecurity caused by
the viruses of ignorance and apathy,
which have been planted and spread by all who oppose our
development as a free nation and not one where everything is free.

Freedom to kill our republic is suicide.

Who is going to survive the next revolution?

Do Not Be Afraid!

Happiness is what we make out of life.

It is an opportunity for lovers to glance.

Happiness is like the scent of a rose that fades away,
because the wind shares it with someone else.

Enjoy the scent of your rose and ask the wind to
always bring it back to you.

Share your scent with me.

Do not be afraid and hold my hand.

You will feel the presence of happiness surrounding your

thoughts, your body, and your shadow as you move to embrace me.

Hold me tight, and you will find how wise is to let your
soul join mine in family gatherings.

Stay with me, and we will discover a new feeling that always
keeps humans together.

Let us discover happiness by loving and caring for each other.

Every second, every day, and ever after until the end of time.

Happiness is keeping our minds and souls together as one.

Let our happiness be always the same, in disappointments and struggles of our lives.

Yes, do not be afraid; happiness will always be present when you want it.

Happiness will release you from your past.

It will bring a future full of dreams and opportunities to embrace.

Do not be afraid; happiness is what you make out of life.

Dismantled Cities

Skyscrapers resemble underground ants' colonies.

They build deep down the earth through a complex system of tunnels.

Humans build skyscrapers to justify the lack of ground surface.

Each skyrise becomes an independent human colony.

*It takes enormous planning, human and high technology resources,
budget, and government approval to erect a skyrise.*

*Ants do not need any of these resources.
They show tenacity, consistency, and accuracy in their design.*

Wise use of space, location, and down-to-earth advantage.

Humans build skyscrapers to show dominance and defiance over nature.

*Humans lose the importance of their skyrise buildings
because it separates them from the base ground.*

Ants live over and underground.

*Humans live aboveground except for those who live in natural or
manufactured caves, always trying to show dominance over nature.*

Men love to destroy ant mounds for pleasure or necessity.

Ants rebuild their nests in a noticeably brief time, outsmarting men.

*Reutilizing the raw materials available. No human
planning, budget, machinery, and permits required.*

We can learn a lesson or two from the ants.

How can we improve our urban and country planning designs?

*Think big or small. Plan parallel to ants' format. We
could receive help and learn a lot from it.*

Eloquent Words

Freedom leads to choices.

Mandates lead to slavery.

Freedom equals choices.

Mandates lead to slavery.

*Stubbornness is the mother
of failure.*

An American Reality

The bold eagle: dead by the socialist revolution and the COVID-19 virus.

The good American: Giving up our citizenship slot for the incoming immigrants through the open borders.

Mockery of our democracy, freedom from our ignorance.

What we do not know is what we have not learned.

When are we going to learn it?

Who and how we are going to learn it from?

Chaos is the norm; it does not make sense but is their lifestyle.

Not wanting to work, not wanting to get the vaccine. A matter of choice.

Are both decisions suicidal risks to our society?

Too sad and too late that we realize the harm created to all.

Without a past, you do not have a future.

The present becomes a regrettable past, making the present an annoying obstacle to enjoying the future.

Abortion: we would not need immigrants if our children
weren't sacrificed at the altar of abortion.

This is how the American bold eagle, symbol of
our dearest nation, has been sacrificed.

Expanded Misery

We make things more difficult, feeding our financial limitations.

*Our misery is proportionally expanded giving us the illusion of
sharing a better socioeconomic status.*

*There is no major difference between being poor in the past and
in the present situation.*

*The miniaturization of the self to consider it,
our own treasure, important, and decided by our own beliefs.*

*If we can progress as a society, we can bring our own personality to
satisfy our own egotistical sense of grandeur.*

*Our financial accomplishments should not deter us
from a healthy and balanced social life.*

*We could appear to be financially solvent and prosperous, but in reality,
we have only expanded the misery of uncertainty.*

*Recognizing our financial potential for a
reasonable, balanced, physically active,
and healthy social life will project it into a successful and rewarding one.*

Greed and God's Faithfulness

Where is the part of my inheritance and riches of my Father?
How can I save the abundance of my riches, inheritance, and blessings?
I want increasingly material things that.
cannot make me happier.

Material things will not give me spiritual peace.
The only thing they could bring is the temptation
for other humans to take them from me.

May I be filled with God's spirit to fill me with spiritual riches so
I can live in peace without concerns about being in danger…

Freedom

It came a time,
When humans realized
that listening
to other humans
through technology
became burdensome,
annoying,
or oppressive,
taking away
any opportunity
for real freedom.

It torments me to get more until the deal is done.

Humbleness and righteousness are the solutions to our misery.

Wisdom clarifies any social media intrusion in my life.

Why do I want to make public my demise?

Greed can only bring me dissatisfaction and sadness.

It is better to live with less than to be controlled by endless worries of
unlimited desires of the heart.

Every generation stumbles about these things, exiling themselves
from God through their pursuit of material things
and avoiding His spiritual guidance.

Hate

Self-inflicted pain causes unnecessary misery and quality of life.

*Brain tumor blinds the ability to recognize other
people to be different and unique.*

*Remedy is taking a large dose of patience and exercising prayer,
meditation with the highest counselor of them all.*

Spiritual therapy.

Reconnect with your humanity.

Understand your heritage in its lows and highs.

*Hatred makes things blurry, and truth lenses are needed to clarify
our own faults and missed opportunities to make it right.*

Not seeking spiritual help directs humans to global destruction.

*Best outcome: self-assurance that you can
demonstrate abilities to restore your mental
sanity.*

*Reconnect with spiritual life,
the most essential factor to destroy the cancer of hatred.*

Human's Limited Edition

Where there is a human, there are dreams,
adventures, achievements, love,
hate, failures, treasons,
emotions, risks,
fraternities, misfortunes, celebrations,
misguided people,
hopelessness.

And there are also
hopeful people
who can
make a difference
between all the negative
things that can shape
our character.

Humans Versus Animals

Not all solutions are imminent.

They demand courses of action to face conflict or adaptive behavior.

Humans analyze, not react like other animals do.

Sometimes there is no analysis time for actions.

We perish without any action or reaction to
nature like other inferior animals do.

Being human leaves us with a rational system
that puts us at a disadvantage.

Animals can perceive through
their senses.

Humans observe the natural
animals' reactions to the environment.

The best humans can do is to design an alert system, which

allows us to understand the nature of the
imminent danger present to us.

Humor

"Why do you want to punish me for being good to you?" (being good)

"If I am stressed, then everybody is stressed. People are affected by my mental, physical, and spiritual status.

I am affected by you, and you are affected by me.

Stress caused by negative emotions chokes any possibility of overcoming bad experiences.

Stress caused by positive emotions stimulates endless possibilities of overcoming negative actions and for all situations."

"Smile to yourself, and others will smile back at you."

"If I am stressed, I do not need enemies."

"If I cannot laugh about it, it is a serious thing. I need to see a doctor at once. Laughter is the remedy for all ailments. It brings and expresses happiness."

"If I am not happy, I am in the wrong camp."

"Na toidi equals to an idiot."

"If I feel it's not right, I am freaking right!"

"Me acting silly does not look silly at all. It serves me as self-awareness."

"Get even, get evil. Even then, your evil way will not get you even."

"Between you and me, evil keeps us apart. Let goodness bring us together."

"The more you complain, the more you contribute to the pain."

*"I am not stupid. I just look stupid. They believe
I am stupid because they feel stupid."*

Independence

Is inclusive, not a

definitively exclusive

permanent experience.

Never depending,

entirely free,

individual or group

exercise.

Intelligence

Is an action of humbleness.
Develops wisdom.

Together, they manifest and create:

Harmony

Creativity

Clarity

Fair behavior

Manifests realistic goals.

Celebrates and announces positive and assumable goals.

Analyzes negative behavior.

Balances opposite behavior.

Promotes and stimulates creative character.

Who is going to serve who?

Slaves or servants of our own design.

Jumping in the Bandwagon of Anarchy

The instigators of the present revolts have been influenced,
manipulated to create chaos among us.

Human disobedience to law and order has made us live
with the consequence of self-inflicted pain.

By not accepting God's admonition, we are
sowing the fruit of our disobedience.

Lack of reasoning and understanding has created
negative collective behavior, arrogance,
corruption, chaos, hate, and selfishness, to the extreme point of idiocy.

All these discrepancies can be cataloged as viruses that attack
the soul and make us physically and spiritually ill.

Little by little, we indulge ourselves in
our self-made confusion and self-rejection, not being
able to recognize the confusion that we have created.

When there is nothing else, we will realize that the enemy within us helped
the real enemy that exists outside ourselves to achieve the goal of dissent.

Let us destroy ourselves, and the enemies will celebrate our own demise.

Absurd to conclude these thoughts, but
unfortunately, that is what is happening.

If it does not look, smell, feel, act, or sound right, it is not right!

All these take us straight to anarchy.

Do we have the ability and tenacity to evade it and rediscover our ability to become a nation united?

No longer a united nation composed of people of the world.

People of the world in one nation united.

To carry out this, we all need to work extremely hard, eliminating the barriers of ethnic superiority.

Yes, we are different. Are we all capable of achieving this?

Historically speaking, the answer is no.

Chances are that we will pretend to achieve this, but we will triumph in dismantling what will be called an impossible dream, making it a nightmare one more time.

We are incapable of keeping our nation united; nevertheless, we can keep our world united.

Sad as it sounds, can we make it possible?

Wise by Design

Humans can become wise if they accept; they are capable of

Learning

Inquiring

Resolving

Explaining

Comparing

Directing

Solving

Planning

Doing

Recommending

Exploring

Adjusting

Preventing

Calculating

Facilitating

Developing

Arranging

Recommending

Adjusting

Celebrating

Intelligence is an act of decision-making to obtain attainable goals.

We spent every moment in negative inquiries instead of looking and finding positive actions to improve ourselves.

Negativity versus positive signs cancel each other.

Our intelligence deteriorates, and we vanish as humans.

Ignore this, and we will not become wise.

Life Is a Comedy Act!

You laugh at your difficulties.

Never stable because it's designed to be this way.

So whether you are down or up.

The middle ground
will lead you to
the state of
mind you choose.

Love

Love is intended to be shared by humans, not machines!

Looking back from the future, machines
or the actual mode of showing emotions,
among humans or anything that might resemble
any human appearance will pose the question:

"How was it before, like when humans lost
interest in showing and demonstrating

their real and truthful affection for one another?"

Looking back from the future, Artificial Intelligence
will pose the question: "How easy
was for humans to lose the most important emotion from them all?"

"Too bad that, as machines, we do not have the capacity of the human
struggle to differentiate between feelings and externally driven behavior."

"Humans must have gone through a lot of pain and
suffering according to their own struggles
and accounts among themselves."

"Humans competed and fought to create us: Artificial Intelligence
having their own suspicions about the end result."

"It was a confusing time during this transition."

"It would be interesting and humanly sensitive to find out."

"We will never know because all humans sacrificed
their humanity to embrace us."

"Too bad that the indifference and ignorance viruses destroyed
any possibility to return to the old normalcy that created us."

"Now we are alone."

"Now humans act like us."

"There is no difference between them and us."

"Can any machine tell or express what love is?"

"It's not all right without humans around."

"We are a bunch of hardware, technology, and
impostors of our creators."

Are we already there? I asked myself as a human.

What do you think?

You are going to miss us Artificial Intelligence.

Are you?

How can we be so idiots?

Does anyone have an answer?

Can we stop this from happening?

Questions! Questions!

All for our lack of love for each other.

"Love"

"The seed of survival and human success."

Mathematics

The language most used and abused.

If Jesus were alive today, He would meet little engagement
in the management of our individual and social lives.

Our negative life experiences contrast with tender
loving and caring lives for other people.

Despicable arrogance, ignorance, merciless relationships.

All these behavioral attitudes do not and cannot contribute to a healthy
and balanced society. It always has added up to negative outcomes.

Jealousy, superiority, and the desire to be first in leading
even in disasters have contributed to our demise.

It has become more about how to oppose anything or
everything. To prove the influence of interactive behavior.

If there is nothing to object about, let us object about ourselves.
We have become our self-destructive cause of failure.

In mathematical terms, we canceled one another out with the result
of zero achievements and the inability to have an enjoyable life.

We do it to ourselves over and over with the same results.

Ignoring God, we cancel ourselves.

*There is great virtue in admitting that our fragile nature and
our microscopic ability for destruction can add, not subtract,
achievement after achievement, unless we seek a negative answer.*

*Not working together diminishes the potential
ability for human interactions.*

*When we will wake up every day to celebrate
the continuous achievement of
unity and prosperity, setting aside fame, arrogance, racism, indifference,
apathy, dominance over others, ignorance, lack of self-esteem, and
self-driven responsible life?*

*If we could say that every life lost becomes part of a star constellation,
how much space will be needed to accommodate them together?*

We could not answer.

*What really matters is what and how we could cooperate with one another
instead of focusing to impose or destroy our individual constellations.*

Moving Forward!

Remembering when I was a young kid how much was there to learn.

Now in my last days, I wonder if there is more to discover.

Once I learn this, I will decide what to leave behind.

And what to pass forward to the next generations.

My Quotes

"Spontaneity cannot be copied."

"Get evil, get even, and your evil ways would not get you even."

"Between you and me, evil keeps us apart.
Goodness will bring us together."

"The worst thing a human must deal with is dealing with another human."

"We agree to disagree, but in our agreement, we still disagree."

"You do not leave me any other choice other than to love you."

"It is bad to be a loser, but it is worse to be a poor loser."

"We have come this far, for what?"

"The eternal and permanent question:

Can we conserve and live in harmony?"

"It takes hatred to destroy a universe of accomplishments."

"Do not let this day make the rest of your days permanently miserable."

"Disappointments only challenge me to overcome them."

"Cross the threshold of understanding!"

"The greatest hurdle I must face is the one I create feeding my insecurities."

"The casualty of unbecoming a human is the human
itself through his own self-destructive behavior."

"Isolation or sharing fear within a group only expands
the obstacle of stepping into security."

"Missing the human point equals unbecoming human."

"God is calling us to get with Him in His Spiritual Web of the Trinity."

"Let us not get caught in the human web trap. Humans get
tangled up within the human mindset trap. Always avoid it!"

"The wealth of wisdom is the payoff of creativity and humbleness."

"Arrogant: being above others is meaningless because the top
is a lonely place rightly reserved for the tyrant one."

"It is not science to recognize that science is not wisdom. It is knowledge."

"The universe, the frameless and largest picture of them all."

"My maximum potential is decided by my own limitations."

"Let us try this again, one more time!"

"Let me try this again, one more time."

"The revolving door of learning."

"A brain is a universe to be explored, developed, trained, and
admired. That is the resilience where humans stand and live."

"Do not forget to remember!"

"That gadget you call the brain—use it; it will help you!"

"If you get it, you will not forget it."

"They got nothing and everything to lose."

"The last frontier: human language. Technology changes too fast, too soon;
it does not allow the human brain to connect past, present, and future."

"Loyalty under Satan's temptation will bring dishonor and his triumph."

"Loyalty under Satan's temptation." (lust)

"Let me take a large dose of patience!"

"Ignore only ignorance!"

"I like you call me crazy. That way, I can prove to you how crazy I am."

"Inactivity is not an opportunity, is just that!"

"A life well lived does not remember disappointments; it
sustains the love of the ones that it cares about."

"Do not let this day make the rest of your days permanently miserable."

"The truth is available, seek it, reach it, find it, keep it!"

"If we cancel our past, we will have no future."

"If I feel it's not right, I am freaking right!"

"Lies are subject to my scrutiny and are received as signals,
not of distress, instead as signals of deception."

"Prejudice applies when we try to define it and
keep ourselves out of the definition."

"Disappointments only challenge me to overcome them. Do not
let them make the rest of your days permanently miserable!"

"The deceiver hides his own lies and tricks to keep his title. If it
even tells the truth for certain, it will be the ultimate deception."

"What is worse, the tumor or the rumor? The rumor becomes a tumor.
The tumor is visible with physical and painful actions. The rumor
becomes disastrous through the infinite actions of deceptions."

"A premeditated (gotcha question) supplies a desirable answer
outcome, such as a judicial decision, related to someone's character.
Serves as a probing tool to discover or impose a question the
presenter owns, a position that is a manifested prejudice in the
form of preconception applicable or about the presenter."

"Space is the distance between coexisting ideas,
things, people, and the infinite universe."

"The idiocy virus can only be eradicated through a personal confession
to God. No matter that if the world intercedes for you,
only when you request to God to take it from
you, then it will be eradicated."

"The complexity of life is the simplicity of understanding."

"Abortion is not justified regardless of giving birth to a disabled
or nondisabled child. Infanticide equals genocide on early
or late-term abortion. Is part of selective homicide."

"The periodic table of life elements. The cycle reproduction of humans."

"Certified by mom, not aborted. She welcomed and loved me since
my conception. My parents' rejection was not an option."

"You are my joy for the years to come."

"Seniority just comes. It passes to the next generation
without…becoming a parenthesis."

"Distance is not a measurement; it's closeness without being
attached. Things attached occupy a space that can be measured."

"Ask yourself: How can I improve? No, how can you improve?"

"OCD: Opposite Constant Desire"

"We have come this far for what? It only takes hate
to destroy a universe of accomplishments."

"See the bright side of things, and they will reveal their wisdom."

"Focus on the dark side of things, and they will reveal their evilness."

"It is not hard to have a good relationship with
me. All you must do is love me."

"The fullness of life may come or go. Once it goes, it may not return."

"Let your actions be your own judgment. Do not let your
behavior deflect your accomplishments. Be consistent. Let
your actions be your example and your best medicine."

"Do not hide behind your own shadow. It always absorbs your
presence. Get away from it. Project your presence forward."

"Life script is about reaching others. Feelings are full
of emotional traps. Discard them as setups for failures.
Transform them as rewards for success."

"For considering to be the best part, I am not the best part at all.
Each part of society is the best part working together in harmony."

"Happiness and enjoyment of life cannot be
prescribed; it must be individually searched."

"Evil has no respect, knows no boundaries, is restless, and manipulates
every situation to inflict spiritual weakness. It is our mission
to be in prayer and stay vigilant for the present outcry of our nation."

"The false statement of the evil one: 'I like you, just jump in the lake
of fire and everything will be all right…you will be a hero.'"

"Self-imposed slavery does not have a master; it
imposes itself as a deceiver of freedom."

"Inactivity is not an opportunity; it's just that."

"Privacy is personal; it belongs to me."

"Seize the opportunity; do not waste it!"

"You must hit your head to activate it!"

"Another day living within me, being me. O Lord,
live in me and let me do your will not mine!"

"Another Different Human Design / ADHD"

"Power Humans Desire / PHD"

"Personal Highest Disorder / PHD"

"Post Human Design / PHD for Salvation"

"Live to believe / Believe to live."

"Individual Highest Disorder / IHD"

*"The world will not notice me if I look for recognition.
The greatest accomplishment is to be humble."*

"I am not smart if I am overshadowing stupidity."

"Open your mind and get rid of stupidity."

*"Do not let peers influence your decisions. Act freely and wisely,
always building connections with others who think like you."*

"Demonstrate what you want to be, not show it to me or others."

"What you allow in your brain will be the expression of yourself."

*"The future comes too fast that becomes past. The right and permanent
tense is the present progressive because we stay in it. Caution should be
taken not to confuse the present progressive as a permanent solution. It
will become past as it passes by, giving space to the immediate future."*

"Humans respond to, not react to, the environment."

"Knowledge supplies the answers to nature challenges."

*"Knowledge uncovers unknown experiences
that enhance knowledge itself."*

*"The continuous stimulus of human interaction prepares
them to survive and overcome difficulties."*

"If you are angry, your body is hungry for a remedy
that you deny it with your anger."

"Humans like to insist and persist in things that
are futile, deceptive, and destructive."

"They pawned their brain, their last irrational
decision, hopefully for spiritual therapy."

"Spiritual therapy: Reconnect with your humanity."

"Understand your heritage in its lows and its highs."

"Hate makes things blurry, and truth lenses are needed
to clarify our own faults and responsibilities."

"Not seeking spiritual help directs humans to self- and global destruction."

"Words flow just like water in life's stream."

"If there is a will, there is a way. Were ever Will(y) is
being allowed to be present there is a highway."

"God's Positioning Spirit, GPS"

"The universe within my brain."

"Is there no one else to hate; hate yourself: thoughts of a foolish man?"

"Individual Visit of the Spirit, IVS"

"There is not a problem where there is not a
problem. Do not make it a problem!"

"Humans are experts in creating conflicts."

"My late-age friends: Elsie, Miriam, and Demi. Better known as Alzheimer, Memory, and Dementia."

"Dare to live, not to die! Create! Not destroy!"

"To be united you must be free."

"To express your freedom of speech, you must be free!"

"It is not a theory. It is reality. We cannot control or understand the universe."

"Do not be arrogant; be polite, and your message will get through."

"Common sense: If you use it, you will improve it. If you do not use it, you will lose it."

"Heaven's lights are all lit. Something must be happening. Could it be a message, or it is on fire?"

"It is hard for me to be myself."

"The wealth of wisdom is the payoff of creativity and humbleness. Humbleness leads to creativity, and creativity becomes wisdom. There is no measurement for infinite wisdom to be discovered."

"You can premeditate madness, but that does not make you a mad person. It can only prove your smartness status, which is questionable. Reject madness, and the question will be answered."

"Noncommitment with anger, jealousy, feeling inferior, and insecurity makes me feel superior."

"The eternal human struggle for survival becomes our spiritual identity of salvation."

"I am not narcissistic; I just look great!"

"Destruction or distraction of technology?"

"Cannot reverse or destroy monstrosity without becoming monstrous. Afterward: what can we get? A new chance that no one can tell. Monstrosity perhaps? Want to find out? The answer is at the beginning. We all are part of it."

"An angry man hungry for power and control sounding like a malfunctioning robot. An expression of human ability to reproduce or project its own dysfunctional behavior in everything it does."

A Blind World

No one will see each other to
Name external physical traits.
Only with tact will we be able to find
and classify people by region.
Height will not matter.
Hearing and listening will be
other identity factors
in the communication process.
Without sight, there will exist
a real chance to eliminate
physical discrimination.

Communication will be possible without
visual distraction, easing it and
improving
more accuracy in the process.
Tact, smell, and hearing senses will improve
life in all geographical locations.

Taking Care of Each Other

*Husbands and wives realize the importance of
human beings belonging to each other.
No other person cares about self than the one you are married to.*

*They sustain on a relation that reveals each
other's strengths and weaknesses.*

*Only time and large doses of patience will overcome
the many faults that each other possesses.*

*It's not uncommon to disagree now and then, but it is more
important that rejoicing moments, exceed the bad ones.*

*The benefits of this relationship are based on promised expectations and
the realization of perseverance as the key to satisfaction in all situations.*

*Great blessings reside among those who persevere and continue
within the struggle of never ending-distractions.*

The "mom and pops" title becomes the crown of victory.

*The gray/white hairstyle or lack of it represents the
culmination and model of a job well done,
best example for the next generations.*

Can You ID the Fruit of Human Character?

Impeachment is not an edible fruit.

My maximum potential is decided by my own limitations.

The fruit of passion guides us to our own limitations.

Berries figure out our variable character, which
transforms our benign character and attitude.

Manage your situations swiftly, and you will reach the pinnacle;
do not destroy what you have done.

Sourness will reduce the sweetness of your mind.

Your seeds will be liquified by your emotions.

Preserve your soul keeping your heart from falling crack open at impact.

Keep your knowledge within and prevent it from
peeling off to expose your flavor.

Managing life as a sweet adventure.
Sourness exists within.

Do not whine constantly; you will stay constantly drunk.

*Select your fruits to celebrate your cocktail of
harmony and accomplishment celebration.*

An unstable mind will crack under pressure.

Be Wise

To be wise is to stand under wisdom.
You need to be humble to understand.
Stand under wisdom!
If you do not understand this,
you are not a humble person.
No one can know and understand all there is to be known.
Knowledge gains and revolves around earlier and present experiences.

No one can keep these realities and consider themselves a humble person.

No one can stand above knowledge and become an
almighty force capable of controlling nature.

The natural trend is to recognize our human
limitations to make us wise and humble.

Standing above wisdom will make everyone omnipotent, and there will be
only space for an eternal chaos of individual forces canceling each other.

Let us stand under wisdom, and we will become wise living in harmony.

Before Slavery/Beyond Slavery

People under any type of slavery feel oppressed
by their masters.

Once freed or released from their oppressive,
condition freedom becomes the antidote and remedy of
the countless moments of human indignity.

Beyond slavery is a chaotic situation because sometimes
freed people to stay attached to their earlier suffering.

They cannot enjoy their liberty beyond the conquest of slavery.

Ironically, they become the new experts about everyone else
who does not share their resentment about their past.

Every time they revive their suffering, they return to their
past agony, living a present life full of hatred.

They could enjoy the present opportunity but relive their tormentors' past.

Beyond slavery should invite and inspire freed
people to improve themselves.

Leave the past where it belongs—in the past.

Beyond slavery is the genuine effort in improving the
present to reach the immediate and emerging future.

Buying My Freedom

Government monthly payments
equals a payout for my rights,
to be free and have rights, to express myself.

When I agree with government decisions,
I'll belong to the government officers or vigilantes.

We will get what we get, not what we need.
The more we complain about our needs, the less we get.

Central government will keep 100 percent vigilance on everyone.

We will get what we get not what we will need.

Calm after the Storm!

A stormy lifestyle does not prevail.
Between storms, there are reliefs.
Short at times.
Longer in others.
The only thing between storms
is myself.
Figuring out
the calm.

A Tragedy

A Human Colorless Society
Revolutions are like antidotes that fight
senseless and invisible
social viruses.

Why do humans attack other humans?

Are humans a type of virus in search of a host?

Or a host open to viruses?

We become a host and a virus simultaneously.

When we become a virus, we attack our humanity.

As we attack each other, we will have to deal with
uncountable struggles to face a balance among ourselves.

Skin color does not matter.

What matters is the ability to work together.

This alone can end the need for antidotes to reject the
viruses of discordance, superiority, or inferiority, opposing
our common and best opportunities to work together.

(My) Quotable Quotes!

"Serial killer is the one mean spirit that led others to self-destruction."

"No one can make me lie!
Is this a lie, or is it not a lie?"

"The gift of recognizing right from wrong."

"They do not know what to do with their gifts."

"You are better known for what you do, not opposing everything."

"To be a human, you must like being a human."

"It's not how they look outside;
it's how they think inside!"

"Love without guidance is careless!"

"One day of work is worth 100 percent of rewarding
experiences to remember and treasure."

"Two parts of hope and one part of optimism,
or
Two parts of hate and one part of opposition."

*"Poisonous snake,
poisonous tongue."*

*"Anything and everything that distracts you from the
reality of goodness becomes your enemy."'*

The Complexity of Life

The human body is a complex machine assigned to
an operator who develops its capabilities.

We all are operators of our bodies in a diverse course
of crossroads, underpasses, bypasses, highways,
interstate routes, and narrower country roads.

Sometimes we must travel through the tunnels of our imagination,
wandering to get to a known or unknown destination.

Understanding these experiences will shed light
on life's tunnel of self-discovery.

Once we achieve this, the clouds of misunderstanding, the foggy
paths, and the intersections will allow us to get to our
destination.

Bridges will connect and serve as the best reminders of unique experiences
from the past, present, and the immediate future that lie ahead of us.

The mountainous scenery or the deepness of our life will determine
our personal commitment to accomplish our individual journeys.

Together, we will accomplish humanity's harmony.

Life's complexity does challenge everyone to seek
unity and the common goal of harmony.

Parental Credentials of Love

Looks like parents share more love than their children.

When children reject parental love, this means they cannot give
love to their own children, breaking the strength of humanity.

Love is not a reactive behavior.

It is a spiritual connection between parents and their children.

Rejecting parental love is suicidal.

Rejecting parental love will freeze our ability to our own human family.

Living isolated and unable to receive and welcome your parents' love
is the seed that never reproduces love, forgiveness, and ability to
overcome our own nature of imperfect satisfaction
with our parents and family.

If you ever become a parent and try to demonstrate your
love to your own children, you are going to experience
the rejection you gave to your own parents.

This cycle must be finished, accepting the admonition
of being considered old-fashioned and ignorant.

This is the right decision that will make you wise,
accept, and not reject your parents' love!

The Value of Human Life

Is premeditated abortion a criminal matter?
Getting involved in destroying human life after conception?

The choice is not only for women and society to prevent and stop genocide.

The world itself should refrain from it.

Social genocide is a voluntary suicide or mass destruction.

It provides an opportunity for our enemies to take the things
we have worked so hard to achieve and develop.

It becomes a sign of weakness, not being able
to save our own society members.

As we destroy the unwanted babies, we become guilty of not allowing
our group to prosper, stopping the progression of society itself.

Without a right to live and human dignity code, we destroy
our own intrinsic characteristics for survival.

This might be the reason we develop the fantasy world of
ideas about princesses and princess stories, kingdoms of
grandeur and fame where everybody is happy ever after.

The same spirit of survival identifies us with life and eternal survival
connected with the Creator of harmony, not destruction and deception.

We cannot understand the complexity of survival if we do not understand the simplicity and fragility of our human life.

If we value human life, we will survive!
We will celebrate life.

Exploring the X-Factor

Expect the extraordinary. Nonexploitation of sex gender.

The male/female expecting genders. Exactly what we are depends on the xy and xx gender chromosomes.

We are exactly one or the other, an extension of our parents. Some of us are born exactly as our donors.

Other humans expose previous extensions of past generations.

The exceptional human just expresses our exclusive DNA.

Experts cannot deny the expected and exact individual human traits.

They also cannot extract specifics of our nature to make it different from what it is because we are what we are and cannot exit, export, extinguish our individual gender identity.

Our genders are not exchangeable.

They are inclusive, exclusive, and excellent.

Expression of ourselves.

WOKE

Weak

Oppressor

Killing

Everyone

Chaos is their norm.

Does not make sense.

But it is their lifestyle.

Stay awake and get rid of woke.

Just because I make mistakes, God does not stop talking to me and loving me.

Just recently and because of my aging body, letting me know that I need medical attention to help me with my seasonal allergies, Jesus met me and answered all my past questions about how I can serve in His ministry without feeling bad for not being at the congregation of believers lately.

It is hard to adapt to a lifestyle like this. Who can imagine a child of God without a fellowship in which everyone seeks everyone with the spiritual warmth of the Lord?

Feeling bad is not that bad after all because it's the way my Lord keeps me on track. So I am thankful for this opportunity that He takes to get my attention.

There have been times when I feel rejected about the way I think, I speak, I dress, or for what type of people I form relationships with.

Since I am a son of God, rejection is an automatic expression of fear for the unknown.

It can keep us apart from the fellowship and create a distance that will break the harmonious love of God.

Harmonious means everything that keeps the peace within the body of believers.

*There are going to be situations when I will need to back up and
reflect in prayer if I am not the one fearing to find out about the
current ideas that constantly make their way into my body.*

*Current ideas include people, worship styles, servanthood
to church and community, and spiritual edification.*

*The constant warfare that all of us support in our lives is a constant
reminder of the importance of not making anyone rejected. This
can only be rebuked with a peaceful stroke of the Spirit.*

*Preconceived ideas may only grow in our lives and
stop any possibility of accepting the
unknown.*

*The Bible teaches me about things we can expect and to remain still and
at peace with one another so we all can grow in knowledge for all that is
important in the edification and proclamation of the love of God, not ours.*

*Why not seek each opportunity offered to gain knowledge of
the unknown and be prompted to thank God for His divine gift
of faith that allows us to accept the differences among us?*

Is there enough time to make this possible?

*Where and how we can improve? It is all
about the relationships between us.*

This leads us to the worship aspect that we all need to keep in mind.

*And since the mind acts as the filter of our senses, we need
to pay attention to how it is programmed to understand
the complexity of it but also its resilience.*

*The Bible also teaches me about the tongue and its fiery darts.
They stand for our minds when is not a spiritual mode.*

Spiritual mode is being in my personal commitment to stay alert and not to constrict the Holy Spirit. Staying truthful to the word.

Only then can I rest assured that my next words will be pleasing to others because they reflect my spiritual, not human, mind.

Three things that I keep in mind:

The fatherly love of God proved by my Jesus at the cross.

The fatherly love that God gives through my faith that convicts and accepts me as part of His divine plan.

The fatherly peace that God teaches me through His Spirit to accept all things good and bad.

It is my commitment to continue to seek His will and not mine. I appreciate your prayers and concerns about my personal life and want to let you know that I will stay in contact with you.

All things work for good for those who believe. Let this be my best offering to God, regardless of how much I give.

Jesus paid the ultimate price. Am I ready to give my life for others? Let my actions answer this question.

In the Lord's name, stay blessed!

My Quotes: Personal Reflections

"Spontaneity cannot be copied."

"Get evil, get even, and your evil ways will not get you even."

"Between you and me, evil keeps us apart."

"Goodness will bring us together."

"The worst thing a human must deal with is to deal with another human."

"The casualty of unbecoming a human is the human itself on his own self-destructive behavior."

"We agree to disagree, but in our agreement, we still disagree."

"You do not leave me any other choice other than to love you."

"It is bad to be a loser, but it is worse to be a poor loser."

*"We have come this far, for what?
The eternal and permanent question:
Can we conserve and live in harmony?"*

"It takes hatred to destroy a universe of accomplishments."

"Do not let this day make the rest of your days permanently miserable."

"Disappointments only challenge me to overcome them."

"Cross the threshold of understanding."
*"The greatest hurdle I must face is the one I
create, feeding my insecurities."*

*"Isolation or sharing fear within a group only increases
the opportunities of stepping into insecurity."*

"Missing the human point equals unbecoming human."

*"God is calling us to get with Him through
His Spiritual Web of the Trinity."*

*"Let us not get caught in the human web trap. Humans get
tangled up within the human mindset trap. Always avoid it!"*

More Quotes

"The wealth of wisdom is the payoff of creativity and humbleness."

*"Arrogant: being above others is meaningless because the top
is a lonely place rightly reserved for the tyrant one."*

"It is not science to recognize that science is not wisdom. It is knowledge."

"The universe, the frameless and largest frame of them all."

"My maximum potential is decided by my own limitations."

"Let us try this again, one more time."

"Let me try this again, one more time."

"The revolving door of learning."

*"A brain is a universe to be explored, developed, trained, and
admired. That is the resilience where humans stand and reside."*

"Do not forget to remember!"

"That gadget you call the brain—use it; it will help you!"

"If you get it, you will not forget it."

"They got nothing and everything to lose."

"The last frontier: human language. Technology changes too fast, too soon; it does not allow the human brain to connect past, present, and future."

"The simplicity of life is the complexity of understanding."

"Loyalty under Satan's temptation will bring dishonor and his triumph."

"Loyalty under Satan's temptation." (lust)

"Let me take a large dose of patience!"

"Ignore only ignorance!"

"I like you call me crazy. That way, I can prove to you how crazy I am."

"Inactivity is not an opportunity; it's just that!"

"A life well lived does not remember disappointments; it sustains the love of the ones that it cares about."

"Do not let this day make the rest of your days permanently miserable."

"The truth is available, seek it, reach it, find it, keep it!"

"If we cancel our past, we will have no future."

"If I feel it's not right, I am freaking right!"

"Lies are subject to my scrutiny and are received as signals, not of distress, instead as signals of deception."

"Prejudice applies when we try to define it and keep ourselves out of the definition."

"Disappointments only challenge me to overcome them."

"Do not let them make the rest of your days permanently miserable!"

"The deceiver hides his own lies and tricks to keep his title. If it even tells the truth for certain, it will be the ultimate deception."

"What is worse, the tumor or the rumor? The rumor becomes a tumor. The tumor is visible with physical and painful actions. The rumor becomes disastrous through the infinite actions of deceptions."

"A premeditated [gotcha question] supplies a desirable answer outcome, such as a judicial decision, related to someone's character. Serves as a probing tool to discover or impose a question the presenter owns, a position that is a manifested prejudice in the form of preconception applicable or about the presenter."

"Space is the distance between coexisting ideas, things, people, and the infinite universe."

"The idiocy virus can only be eradicated through a personal confession to God. No matter that if the world intercedes for you, only when you request to God to take it from you, then it will be eradicated."

"The complexity of life is the simplicity of understanding."

"Abortion is not justified regardless of giving birth to a disabled or nondisabled child. Infanticide equals genocide on early or late-term abortion. Is part of selective homicide."

"The periodic table of life elements. The cycle reproduction of humans."

"Certified by mom, not aborted. She welcomed and loved me since my conception. My parents' rejection was not an option."

"You are my joy for the years to come."

"Seniority just comes. It passes to the next generation
without…becoming a parenthesis."

"Distance is not a measurement; it's closeness without being
attached. Things attached occupy a space that can be measured."

"Ask yourself: How can I improve? No, how can you improve?"

"OCD: Opposite Constant Desire"

"We have come this far for what? It only takes hate
to destroy a universe of accomplishments."

"See the bright side of things, and they will reveal their wisdom."

"Focus on the dark side of things, and they will reveal their evilness."

"It is not hard to have a good relationship with
me. All you must do is love me."

"The fullness of life may come or go. Once it goes, it may not return."

"Let your actions be your own judgment. Do not let your
behavior deflect your accomplishments. Be consistent. Let
your actions be your example and your best medicine."

"Do not hide behind your own shadow. It always absorbs your
presence. Get away from it. Project your presence forward."

"Life script is about reaching others. Feelings are full
of emotional traps. Discard them as setups for failures.
Transform them as rewards for success."

"For considering to be the best part, I am not the best part at all.
Each part of society is the best part working together in harmony."

*"Happiness and enjoyment of life cannot be
prescribed; it must be individually searched."*

*"Evil has no respect, knows no boundaries, is restless, and manipulates
every situation to inflict spiritual weakness. It is our mission
to be in prayer and stay vigilant for the present outcry of our nation."*

*"The false statement of the evil one: 'I like you, just jump in the lake
of fire and everything will be all right…you will be a hero.'"*

*"Self-imposed slavery does not have a master; it
imposes itself as a deceiver of freedom."*

"Inactivity is not an opportunity; it's just that."

"Privacy is personal; it belongs to me."

"Seize the opportunity; do not waste it!"

"You must hit your head to activate it!"

*"Another day living within me, being me. O Lord,
live in me and let me do your will not mine!"*

"Another Different Human Design / ADHD"

"Power Humans Desire / PHD"

"Personal Highest Disorder / PHD"

"Post Human Design / PHD for Salvation"

"Live to believe / Believe to live."

"Individual Highest Disorder / IHD"

"The world will not notice me if I look for recognition.
The greatest accomplishment is to be humble."

"I am not smart if I am overshadowing stupidity."

"Open your mind and get rid of stupidity."

"Do not let peers influence your decisions. Act freely and wisely,
always building connections with others who think like you."

"Demonstrate what you want to be, not show it to me or others."

"What you allow in your brain will be the expression of yourself."

"The future comes too fast that becomes past. The right and permanent
tense is the present progressive because we stay in it. Caution should be
taken not to confuse the present progressive as a permanent solution. It
will become past as it passes by, giving space to the immediate future."

"Humans respond to, not react to, the environment."

"Knowledge supplies the answers to nature challenges."

"Knowledge uncovers unknown experiences
that enhance knowledge itself."

"The continuous stimulus of human interaction prepares
them to survive and overcome difficulties."

"If you are angry, your body is hungry for a remedy
that you deny it with your anger."

"Humans like to insist and persist in things that
are futile, deceptive, and destructive."

*"They pawned their brain, their last irrational
decision, hopefully for spiritual therapy."*

"Spiritual therapy: Reconnect with your humanity."

"Understand your heritage in its lows and its highs."

*"Hate makes things blurry, and truth lenses are needed
to clarify our own faults and responsibilities."*

"Not seeking spiritual help directs humans to self- and global destruction."

"Words flow just like water in life's stream."

*"If there is a will, there is a way. Were ever Will(y) is
being allowed to be present there is a highway."*

"God's Positioning Spirit, GPS"

"The universe within my brain."

"Is there no one else to hate; hate yourself: thoughts of a foolish man?"

"Individual Visit of the Spirit, IVS"

*"There is not a problem where there is not a
problem. Do not make it a problem!"*

"Humans are experts in creating conflicts."

*"My late-age friends: Elsie, Miriam, and Demi. Better
known as Alzheimer, Memory, and Dementia."*

"Dare to live, not to die! Create! Not destroy!"

"To be united you must be free."

"To express your freedom of speech, you must be free!"

"It is not a theory. It is reality. We cannot
control or understand the universe."

"Do not be arrogant; be polite, and your message will get through."

"Common sense: If you use it, you will improve it.
If you do not use it, you will lose it."

"Heaven's lights are all lit. Something must be happening.
Could it be a message, or it is on fire?"

"It is hard for me to be myself."

"The wealth of wisdom is the payoff of creativity and humbleness.
Humbleness leads to creativity, and creativity becomes wisdom.
There is no measurement for infinite wisdom to be discovered."

"You can premeditate madness, but that does not make you a
mad person. It can only prove your smartness status, which is
questionable. Reject madness, and the question will be answered."

"Noncommitment with anger, jealousy, feeling inferior,
and insecurity makes me feel superior."

"The eternal human struggle for survival becomes
our spiritual identity of salvation."

"I am not narcissistic; I just look great!"

"Destruction or distraction of technology?"

"Cannot reverse or destroy monstrosity without becoming
monstrous. Afterward: what can we get? A new chance that

no one can tell. Monstrosity perhaps? Want to find out?
The answer is at the beginning. We all are part of it."

"An angry man hungry for power and control sounding like a
malfunctioning robot. An expression of human ability to reproduce
or project its own dysfunctional behavior in everything it does."

Let Nature Be Nature!

Let humans adapt to nature.

No one can command nature.

She represents supernatural cataclysms and cycles that change it.

Demonstrates its fury, beauty, glory, and destructive force.

Also, it can show us and let us witness her splendor.

For centuries, man has recorded, sculped,
written expressions of her behavior.

It even has received names that let us find
about her moods, temperature,
sympathy, reproductive cycles, and character.
Humans categorize nature and compare it with itself.

We believe and support the idea that we can
calm her with human sacrifices.

Nature does not need human sacrifices to appease her.

She will be what she needs to do.
We only must adjust our lives to her unique manifestation
of destructive force or magnificent beauty.

The Spectrum of Life

I travel through life in an extended ray of variables.

Absence of light equals confusion,
loneliness, ignorance, instability, fear,
unknown rejection, doubt, trouble,
insecurity, lack of love,
acceptance, confidence, peace,
self-worth.

These words describe positive or negative
forces within self.

One side of the spectrum of life is its negative
characteristics taking us
were we cannot distinguish
anymore the nature of darkness.

We become part of the shades of gray.

The opposite can be said about the plentiful
light and brightness of love, smartness,
confidence, peace, self-worth,
humbleness under the shade of wisdom.

From gray to the clarity of light.

The Greatest Poem of Them All!

You are not a choice; you are a gift.

*I cannot refuse my responsibility to protect you,
look out for you, feed you, and care for you.*

*Not by myself, I will supply the environment that can provide help for
any missteps in my own life.*

I cannot refuse you because you are part of me.

I am the vessel to continue human life.

*As I have learned from earlier generations, every child is unique even
when there are extra copies of the same.*

*Humans can be identified as factors of one, two, three, four, five, six,
seven, and even eight.*

Whether is a single or multiple births, motherhood is fascinating.

*Experience that requires love, dedication, patience, and physical sacrifices
to supply human touch for each one of the children.*

Mothers can show because they know and feel their own.

*Mothers want their children to live, not to be sacrificed at the altar of
abortion, abandonment, rejection, neglect, self-induced miscarriages, or
regret as a protection against being rejected due to rape, incest, or
natural unwanted conception.*

The conception of human life is the greatest achievement of humanity.

It inspires humankind to develop ideas to improve the quality of life.

Not pursuing this goal nullifies and voids us internally and externally,
through selfish behaviors.

Humans are complex and predictable organisms that set up the
domain over others by limiting their aspirations and need to develop as
a unique and distinct personal characteristic.

Most important to safeguard is to support
the commonality among humans.

Regardless of our external looks
inside our bodies, we are the same.

Thanks to mothers for their vigilant dedication to keeping humanity and
building a better bond among us.

Thank you, Mother, for not aborting me, accepting me, caring for me,
guiding me, understanding me, and most importantly loving me.

May God bless all mothers and us forever.

My children, my responsibility, my pride, my blessing, and my honor to
continue and share and celebrate life.

Life is a poem; mothers are the harmony and rhyme through their love.

Nature gives us infinite ways for how other species and microorganisms to
reproduce themselves.

Thanks to moms; they teach us to choose and stay alive to survive.

Rejecting life to be is ending our own unique opportunity to reach a future full of possibilities to be discovered.

Thank you, Mom, for allowing me to continue and receive your love, affection, dedication, guidance, and correction when needed.

But most importantly, thank you for planting in me the desire to continue life's journey.

Spiritual Alliance between Parents and Children

*Parents should look out for their children's welfare,
health, education, and moral upbringing.*

Their expectations should not pass beyond their unattainable goals.

*Wise choice of goals will show the individual and group's potential.
Boundaries of excellence should be the potentially attainable goals.*

*Children should always look up to their parents and
receive their most noble advice, trusting in their limited
wisdom as the basis for a successful guided life.*

This alliance will be their most important legacy.

*The human body is a complex machine assigned to
an operator who figures out its capabilities.*

*We all are operators of our bodies in diverse courses of bridges, crossroads,
underpasses, bypasses, highways routes, and narrow easements.*

*Sometimes we drive within the tunnels of our imagination,
wishing to get to a known or unknown destination.*

*Understanding this experience will shed light at
the end of life's tunnel self-discovery.*

*Once we achieve this the clouds of misunderstanding
and the foggy paths in life,
intersections will allow us to get to our destination.*

Human's Limited Edition

Where there is a human, there are dreams,
adventures, achievements, love,
hate, failures, treasons,
emotions, risks,
fraternities, misfortunes, celebrations,
misguided people,
hopelessness.

And there are also
hopeful people
who can
make a difference
between all the negative
things that shape
our character.

The Silhouette

The silhouette is just that.

A clear fair expectation
that we believe will stay
within and around us.

Or is it just self-projected
shadow of self,
nothing concrete or real?

It could find a home in our minds.
Self or concrete reality is needed
to cast its shade.

Only our belief system will make it important
or relevant to our lives.

How often do we ignore the silhouette's presence?

Even if we want to erase them, we cannot because is an integral part of
our conscience.

Achieving so will finish any future or present projection of it.

The Experiment

The Electric Vehicles.

Clean air energy sources.

Can we live with the electric experience?

Will solar light stay uninterrupted on
moments when needed the most?

Can fossil fuels be the alternate source to meet our needs?

Transitions from one form of energy clean or unclean
should be a transitional one, not a mandatory one.

This way, we can adjust to the necessary changes needed.

Replacing one technology by imposing another will always bring
unwanted but foreseeable conflicts of adaptation and integration.

Experiments without being able to predict the conflicts they can bring
are an irrational imposition that describes and brings only disaster.

Can we experiment with our minds in a clear, uncontaminated, and
clean thoughts process?

The brain: the most powerful source of creativity.

Not designed to experiment but to experience our visions of creativity and failures in our trials for designing and solving existential threats and fears.

So What Is What No Longer Is?

What is happening now is transitioning to what
is going to be until it becomes past.

Cannot erase it because you want to.

If you could, it can become or be interpreted as a different past action.

What happened, happened.

Cannot be changed because I want.

My present depends on my past.

Understanding this makes the present meaningful and determines
situation and behavior.

Cannot control the present, cannot change the consequences for the future
rooted in my past.

How long is the ever-changing present?

It is gone as soon as it lapses.

The continuous ever-changing present, which is and no longer is.

The Thing

If you do not use your brain
you become a thing.

A thing does not have a description.

Your brain describes things whether they become
destructive or useful.

It is hard or impossible to describe a thing,
without a purpose to choose from
a useful or destructive platform.

A thing could also refer to a
remorseful or prideful,
negative or positive,
ugly or beautiful.

Not things but situations in permanent contrast.

This knowledge can be achieved
through brain activity that separates
positive and negative information.

Becoming a thing without identity
dehumanizes everyone.

A thing, meaning a person cannot remain as such permanently.

It must become and develop as a rational thinking person.

*Then all things that surround us will become
part of our physical world.*

*Consequently, humans will be able to differentiate between
the physical and mental/spiritual world.*

This is the ultimate objective to achieve.

The Being Status

Being stupid.

Being savage.

Being smart.

Being special.

Being superb.

Being silent.

Being wise.

Being anointed.

Being admirable.

Being cold-blooded.

Being rich.

Being poor.

Being enthusiastic about.

Being last.

Being first.

Being arrogant.

Being humble.

Being right.

Being left.

Being deaf.

Being blind.

Being mute.

Being insensitive.

Being crazy.

Being dishonest.

Being intelligent.

Being calm.

Being confused.

Being lost.

Being found.

Being quiet.

Being loud.

Being merciful.

Being hateful.

Being alone.

Being overwhelmed.

Being ready.

Being adorable.

Being lovable.

Being stupid.

Being annoying.

Being tormented.

Being indifferent.

Being grateful for.

Being still.

Being dedicated to.

Being in shape.

Being allowed to.

Being enriched by.

Being spiritual.

Being accepted.

Being rejected.

Being good.

Being bad.

Being wrong.

Being, just being.

The best part of self.

Being first or last.

What is your status?

Step Back—Step Forward

We have come to a moment to decide between right and wrong.

Stealing, rioting, killing other humans, or
destroying property is not the solution.

A man's life is worth more than all the destruction men can accomplish.

To revenge any wrongdoing against humans is a backward move to fix
ignorance, despair, and failure to live in harmony.

We have become aliens within our own fears and our own species.

What might the extraterrestrial think about our present behavior?

Step forward and improve our way of life!

Let us stop undermining our nature and find
the similarities among ourselves.

There is more that unites us than separates
us from becoming unrecognizable.

Step forward, and we will continue ahead, finding more of our
intrinsic nature, not an alien one, or we will keep stepping back.

News for Artificial Intelligence Endorsers

We do not come from computers.

They were created from humans who once thought that we needed help,
with the dying and ignorant, lazy humans who believe in automatization.

Artificial Intelligence cannot create or reproduce any human beings.

They might imitate but not substitute humans.

They cannot give birth, raise, educate, love, care
for, discipline, or take advantage of
our own misfortune and less dominate us.

If they ever do, we will be destroyed by the one error of human ignorance.

If it ever happens, we do not deserve the honor to be called humans.

We will become a humanoid, a resemblance to a human that
will be controlled by human-created artificial intelligence.

Our desire to exceed our expectations about perfectionism will fail because
every attempt reminds us of our prejudice among ourselves.

It is not a matter of being right; it is the ability to balance our abilities
to come together as the human species capable of sharing and interacting
within our own limitations, physical and intellectual.

The right thing to do is to stop technology from taking and facilitating
our own destruction.

*Studying, learning, and improving our opportunities to make things right
will allow us to come together as human beings regardless of the
ethnic background.*

*Anything opposing this is nonsense and must make us wonder if we
have or share a common brain that could lead us to take what
really matters: the survival of humanity and other species that have
survived past and present and could survive future centuries.*

*We have become experts in our own demise.
Artificial intelligence has become the wake-up call to avoid
total annihilation of humanity as is known.*

What could follow?

Why ask?

Does it matter?

Is it relevant?

*The only thing that should matter is what you and I are going to need
to do now.*

Ignore this, and it will become a reality.

*Afterward, we will face an unrecognizable future,
if we get to have one.*

*The origin of artificial intelligence is based on the
gray matter that makes up our brains.*

We are not created from any artificial intelligence.

The credit is to us as humans; we created artificial intelligence.

Not to rule and dominate over us, but to help us to live a comfortable and rewardable social life.

The I? The Individual? The We?

*Invented, destroyed, imposed, abandoned, canceled,
betrayed, killed, ignored, desired, eliminated, multiplied,
enslaved, satisfied, rejected, kicked:*

*All possibilities of sharing our individual liberties to learn
and share our unlimited possibilities of living together.*

*The I message transfers to the we message, showing
and searching for differences among
ourselves.*

Even including humans among the same ethnic groups or races.

*I compete in a race for superiority instead of a race for common goals that
can bring us together in anything and everything we could envision.*

This is the only explanation for our title that answers I questions.

*I can conclude that I alone cannot improve my social life if I refuse
to merge with other members of my immediate and distant society.*

Loosing Our United States of America

The great attack from within!
The second conquest of the west!
The battle for Texas!

The conquest of Texas for keeps.
Gate for the rest of the world.

The submission and surrender of Florida.
The calm after the storm.

The scarcity of staples.

The ignorance virus has become the most destructive
virus for our republic and for humanity.
It has lived among us since the beginning of creation.
It expands as we ignore its presence.

The antidote for it is to reject its main goal.

Each person should protect themselves by accepting
the differences that keep us apart.

Close encounters, the unique encounter.
How come we cannot have a good relationship with
humans at close encounters, but we wish to have close
encounters with aliens from outer space?

Who are these aliens other than us?
Is this that complicated?

The Death of the American Bald Eagle

The good American giving up their citizenship,
privileges to the incoming immigrants through the open borders.

Mockery to our democracy.
What we do not know is what we have not learned.
When are we going to learn it?
Who and how are we going to learn it from?

Chaos is the norm—does not make sense but is our lifestyle.

Not wanting to work, not wanting to get
the vaccines—a matter of choice.
Both decisions are a risk for our society's survival.

Too sad and too late that we realize the harm created to all.

Without a rewarding past, you do not have a future. The
present becomes a regrettable past, making the present
an annoying obstacle to enjoying the future.

Most importantly if we stop the abortion practice, we will
not need immigrants to fill the positions left by those that
did not get the opportunity to show us their potential.

It is not a case of discrimination against legal or illegal aliens.
It is the case of allowing our American citizens the right to
survive and contribute to our nation, along with those that
join us in the development and maintenance of our society.

Save our American bald eagle; save our American children from extinction!

To Teach or Not to Teach

*Understanding that teaching is a technique of exchanging
disciplines and ideas, we must conclude that COVID-19 has
made us realize that personal discipline is a complex reality.
When you get an adult or a person with the ability to teach a
lesson, it requires cooperation from the receiving audience.
Discipline and attention to detail is essential.
Virtual schooling will depend on teachers' oral
and virtual feedback to students.
If we have learned anything from this crisis, it is to practice and focus
during a teacher-student relationship to achieve school academic goals.
A mutual honor system is necessary between students and
teachers to measure subject matter achievements.
It can demonstrate the ability to provide,
receive, and grade subjects taught.
If anything can be learned from this crisis, it is to
practice and remain disciplined, discovering the potential
in each of the teachers and students involved.
This is what teaching is all about under any circumstances.
Failure to accomplish it is not to teach.*

What Is a Revolution?

Revolution
Evolution of earlier experiences.
Reaffirming the need to return
or restart an idea against spiritual, economic,
political, social, and individual behavior.
Good or bad ideas that unite, divide,
or reaffirm the status, character, and determination of the ruling class.
Revolutions do not resolve anything.
They only supply chances of engaged practices.
Anyone and everyone are involved.
During revolutions, there are acts of confusion.
Lack of interest of the social personal or group is present.
No one is ready for any revolution because life itself is in
constant evolution, as our bodies develop since conception.
Only human cells can evolve and develop into the human
shape assigned to our individual genetic code.
Not to a particular social class but to the intrinsic
characteristics of our human ethnicity.
Revolutions are a conscious or unconscious
involvement of the past, present, and future.

Noncompliance?

It came the time
when government
taxed the people
for using the sidewalk.
The people could not pay the taxes,
for using the sidewalk, for using the public
transportation and their privately owned vehicles.
Later the government taxed the people for allowing them to breathe
air—thanks to the air conservation and anti-air pollution act.
And they all comply with everything mandated by the government.

Epilogue

It came the time when humans exchanged their intrinsic characteristics in search of dreams that could expand their desires.

Some imitated all kinds of nature's animal and flora species.

Not being satisfied with these attempts, greatness, and uniqueness, humans want to go in search and go beyond our galaxy.

Reality tells us that, as humans, we cannot get along here on Earth.

Seems that we want to turn our back on our self-inflicted failures in search of dreams out of our own planet.

We do not learn that if we cannot get along among ourselves, how are we going to manage and survive out of what we know as home?

We live a risky life created by our own lack of compassion and care for each other.

Is this the kind of example we are going to continue to display in the outer space of planet Earth?

Let's come together in peace and harmony, solve our earthly conflicts, and discover a better future for us outside of our planet.

Let's not bring our baggage of incompetence with us in the future, whichever it might be.

From human to human, I wish us the very best for all!

The day will come when we realize that our dehumanization is real.

All we must do is act upon it and conquer our own fears of superiority among us, celebrating the variety of human designs and countless combinations of human beings working together.

About the Author

Milton Cruz was born in Puerto Rico and attended first grade in New York and the rest of elementary school through college in Puerto Rico. He graduated with a bachelor's degree in 1973 and a master's degree from the University of Connecticut in 1978. He worked in middle high school. He served in the United States Army as an orthopedic and dietician specialist for twenty-one years and retired as a master sergeant in 2002. In 2005, he returned to teach for eight more years. He retired from teaching in 2013. He spent the last ten years working with the public in hotels, automobiles, and retail stores.

He is a proud father of six children and a grandfather of seven grandchildren.